Home Office Research Study 228

At the margins:
drug use by vulnerable young
people in the 1998/99
Youth Lifestyles Survey

Chris Goulden and Arun Sondhi

The views expressed in this report are those of the authors, not necessarily those of the Home Office (nor do they reflect Government policy).

Home Office Research, Development and Statistics Directorate
November 2001

Home Office Research Studies

The Home Office Research Studies are reports on research undertaken by or on behalf of the Home Office. They cover the range of subjects for which the Home Secretary has responsibility. Other publications produced by the Research, Development and Statistics Directorate include Findings, Statistical Bulletins and Statistical Papers.

The Research, Development and Statistics Directorate

RDS is part of the Home Office. The Home Office's purpose is to build a safe, just and tolerant society in which the rights and responsibilities of individuals, families and communities are properly balanced and the protection and security of the public are maintained.

RDS also part of National Statistics (NS). One of the aims of NS is to inform Parliament and the citizen about the state of the nation and provide a window on the work and performance of government, allowing the impact of government policies and actions to be assessed.

Therefore –

Research Development and Statistics Directorate exists to improve policy making, decision taking and practice in support of the Home Office purpose and aims, to provide the public and Parliament with information necessary for informed debate and to publish information for future use.

First published 2001

Application for reproduction should be made to the Communications and Development Unit, Room 201, Home Office, 50 Queen Anne's Gate, London SW1H 9AT.

© Crown copyright 2001   ISBN 1 84082 763 7
ISSN 0072 6435

Foreword

This report presents an analysis of data from the 1998/99 Youth Lifestyles Survey (YLS), focusing upon levels of drug use by vulnerable young people such as serious and persistent offenders, rough sleepers, serial runaways and school truants and excludees. All were found to have high rates of drug use. It also considers access to drugs and patterns of drug-related behaviour and offending in comparison with other young people.

The YLS offers a rare opportunity to see information on drug use by marginalised groups of young people, whilst at the same time being statistically representative of the general population in England and Wales. The data presented in this report are an important adjunct to the main measures of drug use obtained from the British Crime Survey (BCS) and the national Schools Survey. Several projects on vulnerable groups have also been recently commissioned in support of the Government's anti-drugs strategy.

The high levels of drug use among vulnerable groups reported here justify the continued focus in the strategy on targeting drugs prevention and education efforts at young people encountering difficulties at school, at home and with the law. More in-depth analyses will shed further light on drug use and access to services among these young people when the projects within the Vulnerable Groups Research Programme report during 2002/03.

David Pyle
Drugs and Alcohol Research Unit
Research, Development and Statistics Directorate

Acknowledgements

The authors would like to thank Charlie Lloyd (Joseph Rowntree Foundation), Ziggy MacDonald (Leicester University) and Mike Shiner (Goldsmiths College, University of London) for acting as independent assessors for this report.

The advice, guidance and support of Malcolm Ramsay throughout the duration of this project have been invaluable. Thanks are also due to Siobhan Campbell, Victoria Harrington and G.D.K. Kinshott in the Research, Development and Statistics Directorate of the Home Office for their advice and assistance with regard to data and analysis issues.

The work of the National Centre for Social Research in designing the 1998/99 YLS and carrying out the fieldwork is gratefully acknowledged, and particularly the work done by Jon Hales and Nina Stratford in preparing the YLS Technical Report.

Chris Goulden
Arun Sondhi

Contents

Summary

The Government has commissioned various pieces of research, such as the BCS, that monitor and help to explain drug use among young people. These are essential in tracking the broad outcomes and planning the strategies of drug policy but do not currently produce reliable guides to drug use among more marginalised sections of society.

Certain groups have repeatedly been identified in research as being prone to the risk factors associated with problematic drug use (e.g. early initiation into drug and alcohol use or living in deprived areas). These 'vulnerable groups' of young people include those who are homeless or involved in offending, for example.

Currently, research into drug use by these groups in the United Kingdom is a largely neglected area and there are few reliable data on their rates of drug use at a national level. In contrast, this report presents the results of secondary analyses of drug use by four vulnerable groups in the YLS. This survey was carried out during 1998/99 with a representative sample of almost 5,000 young people in England and Wales aged 12 to 30.

The four vulnerable groups considered in this report are:

- school truants and excludees
- young offenders
- homeless young people and runaways
- young people living in drug-using families

A summary of the chapters concentrating on each of these groups follows.

School truants and excludees (Chapter 2)

Among the sub-sample of young people aged 12 to 16 in the YLS, there were higher rates of drug use for truants and those excluded from school compared with those routinely attending school. This implies that school-based surveys of drug use will produce slight underestimates of prevalence (as these pupils are less often in class to complete school surveys).

About half of truants and excludees had ever used any illicit drug but only 13 per cent of attenders had ever done so. Use of drugs within the last year was similar for truants and excludees, but seven per cent of excludees were using a Class A drug at least monthly compared with only a fractional proportion of truants (and no attenders reported doing so).

The prevalence of drug use was generally higher for female than for male truants and excludees, although there was no statistical difference in the use of more harmful drugs, such as heroin and crack. In fact, drug use may be one of the reasons why pupils have been excluded from school initially. Drugs prevention research could usefully target young excludees and truants to determine what interventions might be appropriate for them, and particularly whether specific strategies are required for female non-attenders.

Young offenders (Chapter 3)

The links between criminal offending and drug use are reasonably well established, although the nature of these links and how they interact are less clearly known. The YLS provides a representative sample of young offenders 'at large' and not drawn, as is often the case, entirely from criminal justice or treatment sources.

Young offenders are categorised into three groups:

- serious and/or persistent offenders (committing three or more minor offences and/or at least one serious offence in the last year)
- minor offenders (committing one or two minor offences in the last year)
- non-offenders (never committed any offence)

Three-quarters of serious and/or persistent offenders had used an illicit drug in their lifetime and nearly three-fifths had done so in the last year. This compares with a quarter and one-seventh respectively for non-offenders. Rates of cocaine use within the last year were around 12 times higher for offenders compared to non-offenders. Serious and persistent male offenders were four times more likely to be using Class A drugs on at least a monthly basis than their female counterparts. These levels are, however, low compared with those reported by (perhaps more prolific and serious) offenders arrested by the police or incarcerated.

Homeless young people and runaways (Chapter 4)

Homelessness can take many forms and some young people are particularly at risk of becoming homeless in the volatile period after leaving home or local authority care. Homeless young people are also prone to complicating and inter-related problems such as mental and physical illnesses, learning difficulties, disablement, offending and substance dependence.

The YLS only asked respondents about past episodes of homelessness (the YLS being a household survey), including whether respondents had ever slept rough. Nearly four per cent (aged 16 to 30) had been homeless for a month or more and just over one per cent had slept rough (only 38 people in the sample). Eighty per cent of those who had ever slept rough had tried an illicit drug, compared with 53 per cent of those who had never been homeless. One in ten of the 'rough sleepers' were using a Class A drug at least monthly during the previous year.

Multiple childhood attempts at running away from home can often result from experiences of abuse and be a precursor to later periods of homelessness. YLS respondents were asked whether they had run away from home for one or more nights when they were under 16 without telling their parents or guardians where they were and the total number of times they had done so. Almost six per cent had run away from home, and of these, one in seven had also been homeless – this compares with only one in fifty of those who had never run away.

Over 80 per cent of serial runaways (i.e. those fleeing home more than once) had ever used illicit drugs, compared with 42 per cent of young people who had never run away from home. One in twelve serial runaways were using a Class A drug at least monthly over the last year. Homeless and runaway females had relatively higher prevalence rates compared to their non-vulnerable counterparts, although males had the highest absolute rates.

Increased prevalence of drug use seemed to persist into later life for these young people, even when episodes of homelessness or running away occurred some time in the past. It must be remembered, though, that the young homeless are not a homogeneous mass and consequently, risk factors, mental health and substance use will all vary within this group.

Living in drug-using families (Chapter 5)

The context in which young people grow up, in terms of their relationships with and the drug use of siblings, parents and peers, has been shown to affect the initiation and extent of their drug use. The YLS sample was based on households included in the 1998 BCS and some of the respondents were therefore different members of the same family, living together. The two datasets were linked via a unique household identification number and combined to compare drug use between parents and their children and between siblings.

Drug use by parents was rare, although similar to rates for comparable age groups. Only three per cent had used an illicit drug in the last year and 21 per cent had ever done so (mostly cannabis on both counts). Compared to the other vulnerable groups, association in drug use across generations was weak. This was perhaps because recent drug use by parents was restricted to cannabis, reflecting parenthood's role as an acknowledged protective factor. Children may also have been more willing to admit to their own drug use if they knew their parents to be occasional cannabis smokers, for instance, potentially biasing reports.

The sibling data pointed to further contrasts, where recent use by older siblings was associated with higher rates among their younger brothers and sisters. The rates of drug use by those with an older sibling who had never used drugs were very low indeed, at three per cent for lifetime use of any drug, for instance.

Conclusion (Chapter 6)

The levels of use and ease of access to drugs were consistently higher for vulnerable groups, although it was not always possible to control for other potentially confounding factors. Where this was done, in terms of age and gender, the relationships usually remained.

Indeed, an important finding from this analysis has concerned the interaction between gender and 'vulnerability', particularly among the younger groups of truants and excludees. For instance, rates of drug use among excludees – the more disaffected of the two groups – were invariably higher for girls than for boys.

Although the analyses are unable to resolve whether higher prevalence of drug use leads to dependent/problematic use, comparatively heavy drug use at a young age can often be a warning signal. Indeed, the vulnerable groups examined here often had higher levels of monthly use of a Class A drug in comparison with more mainstream young people. More detailed surveillance of drug use in this population, tracking their behaviour as they grow older, is recommended.

This report helps to extend knowledge of patterns of drug use by vulnerable youth. It is intended to inform the Government's anti-drugs strategy and provide additional background for an ongoing programme of quantitative and qualitative research, concentrating on particular vulnerable groups, which reports in 2002. The tracking of the performance of the Government's anti-drugs strategy should continue to include a focus on groups of young people at particularly high risk of developing problematic drug use.

1   **Introduction**

The misuse of drugs by young people has become an increasingly high-profile issue for social policy and society in general over the last decade. This is reflected in the Government's anti-drugs strategy, *Tackling Drugs to Build a Better Britain*, which has a key objective to "help young people resist drug misuse in order to achieve their full potential in society" (UKADCU, 2000). In order to track levels of drug use among young people, the Government has commissioned various national surveys utilising robust methodologies (in particular, the BCS and a regular drugs survey in English schools). These surveys monitor broad changes in the extent and nature of drug access and use among young people. However, whilst these indicators are essential in tracking the broad outcomes of Government policy, they do not provide reliable guides to drug use among more marginalised groups of young people.

There is a growing interest at all levels in matters pertaining to social exclusion, deprivation and vulnerability to problematic drug use that cuts across issues surrounding the prevalence of drug use among young people in general. Certain groups are repeatedly identified as being especially prone to the development of multiple risk factors associated with problematic drug use (HAS, 1996; Lloyd and Griffiths, 1998; Evans and Alade, 2000). These risk factors include such indicators as early initiation into drug and alcohol use (Hall, 2000) or living in a socially deprived area (RCP, 2000). The 'vulnerable groups' of young people identified in previous research include those (HAS, 1996):

- looked after or supervised by local authorities
- who are homeless or local authority care leavers
- involved in offending, including those involved in the criminal justice system
- with drug or alcohol misusing parents
- disaffected from or excluded from school
- living in difficult family circumstances, including those subject to abuse

Furthermore, the Government's anti-drugs strategy suggests that "for early to mid-teenagers, there are strong links between drugs problems, exclusion or truancy from school, break-up of the family and initiation into criminal activity" (UKADCU, 1998: p.14). Clearly, however, these vulnerable groups are not discrete entities and young people may shift between them over time and in association with variations in the nature of their drug use. Indeed, they may be in one or more vulnerable groups concurrently – for example, a young, looked after person, excluded from school and appearing before a magistrate on a shoplifting charge.

Currently, research into substance use by vulnerable young people in the United Kingdom is a largely neglected area and there are few reliable data on the prevalence of drug use within these groups. A rapid R&D programme funded by the Department of Health has, however, recently provided some valuable initial insights (Evans and Alade, 2000). Much of the previous work on young people experiencing social difficulties with the law, their families and/or at home and school has been conducted elsewhere – mostly in the USA. Furthermore, on the rare occasions on which such studies have been done in this country, they have been restricted to a small number of locations (e.g. Powis et al., 1998). In contrast, this report presents results on drug use among selected vulnerable groups from secondary analysis of the national 1998/99 YLS.

The Youth Lifestyles Survey

The 1998/99 YLS was a self-report, household survey of young people, examining the extent and nature of offending within a lifestyle context. It consisted of a representative sample of 4,848 young people aged 12 to 30 living in England and Wales and was carried out for the Home Office by the National Centre for Social Research. The survey interviews were conducted between October 1998 and January 1999 (for further information on the survey, see Stratford and Roth, 1999). This was the second sweep of the survey, following the 1992/93 YLS, which achieved a sample of 2,529 young people aged 12 to 25. For the full report on the first YLS, see Graham and Bowling, 1995 and for the 1998/99 survey, see Flood-Page et al., 2000. Direct comparisons between the two surveys are difficult, since different data collection methodologies were used in each and, in any case, are beyond the scope of this report.

The 1998/99 YLS sample was generated from the 1998 BCS, which sampled individuals aged over 16 living in private households but also captured information on non-interviewees living there. Of 14,947 BCS households interviewed in 1998, 5,117 were eligible for inclusion in the YLS core sample, of which 3,643 led to successful interviews (a response rate of 71%). A further 6,884 addresses next door to the BCS sample households were contacted (a process known as 'focused enumeration') with weighting towards high-crime areas. These households contained 1,895 addresses with at least one person aged between 12 and 30, of which 1,205 (64%) were interviewed as a booster sample for the YLS. In total, the response rate for the whole sample was 69 per cent. Given this response rate, caution should be applied to the findings in this report, as those disposed towards drug use and offending could be more likely to refuse to take part or less likely to be available for interview in either the BCS or YLS. Previous research on the BCS (Aye Maung, 1995) has suggested a non-response bias skewed towards households within high-crime areas, which may lead to under-reporting of drug use and offending behaviours.

Developing estimates of drug use

The YLS, with its wide range of lifestyle questions, has the potential to examine the scope and types of young people who may be vulnerable to drug use from a sample representative of the general population of England and Wales. It has been possible to extract information on school excludees and truants, young offenders, those who had ever been homeless or run away from home and, in combination with the 1998 BCS, drug use within families living in the same households.

Data from self-report surveys, such as the YLS and BCS, provide a fairly accurate enumeration of *general* patterns of drug use within the mainstream population, on a lifetime and last-year basis (Aye Maung, 1995). However, we are only able to provide a limited assessment of *problematic* use. This is usually defined as those who experience "… social, psychological, physical or legal problems related to intoxication and/or regular excessive consumption and/or dependence as a consequence of his own use of drugs or other chemical substances (excluding alcohol and tobacco)" (ACMD, 1982: p.34).

The YLS is a household survey and, in this setting, patterns of problematic drug use, however defined, are comparatively rare and even more rarely obtained. Household or school surveys are unlikely to capture fully the more highly problematic and persistent types of drug user and their patterns of drug use. This is partly because of the under-reporting of more recent and frequent drug use in general and of drugs with the greatest social stigma attached – heroin in particular (White and Lewis, 1998; Hoyt and Chaloupka, 1994; ACMD, 1998). Household surveys are also less likely to capture those with more chaotic lifestyles associated with problematic drug use (Egginton and Parker, 2000), either because they are homeless (however defined), less willing to take part, or less likely to be available for interview. Nonetheless, household surveys can be used, albeit with low thresholds, to identify some fairly problematic types of drug misuse (e.g. the Psychiatric Morbidity Survey). Data from this survey (quoted in ACMD, 1998), for instance, have highlighted the discrepancies in reported drug use between household, institution-based and homeless samples. Here, lifetime use of any drug among young people living in institutions was twice as high, and among homeless people six times as high, than in the household survey. Although those living in institutions make up less than one per cent of the total population of 12- to 30-year-olds, the findings presented here will nevertheless under-represent the true picture of drug use among vulnerable groups. Previous experience of homelessness or imprisonment is, however, examined in this report.

A potential indicator of the risk of progression to dependent use is evidence of frequent and regular consumption of drugs, especially those defined as having greater potential for harm in the 1971 Misuse of Drugs Act (i.e. Class A drugs). In this report, we have included 'use of any Class A drug at least once per month over the last year' as a statistic in most of the tables presented. The frequency of use over the last year is given for cannabis and the Class A drugs enquired of in the YLS in Table 1.1 below.

Table 1.1: *Percentage of respondents reporting different frequencies of use of cannabis and the major Class A drugs during the last year (aged 12 to 30)*

	Once or twice this year	Once every couple of months	Once a month	Two or three times a month	Once or twice a week	Three to five days a week	Every day	Unwtd. (n)
Cannabis	35	14	6	12	12	7	13	1,059
Class A Drugs								
Cocaine	59	18	10	6	4	0	3	176
Crack	47	7	20	13	0	0	13	19
Ecstasy	41	26	10	15	5	-	3	182
Heroin	46	5	0	0	14	14	23	23
LSD	62	14	11	4	2	2	5	85
Methadone	40	10	0	10	0	0	40	9
Mushrooms	81	7	4	2	3	2	2	88

Source: YLS weighted data. Unweighted numbers are for those who reported using the drug in the last year for the entire sample; those who did not use a drug in the last year are excluded from the table. '-' = less than 0.5%.

This shows, that one in four heroin users and one in seven cannabis users were taking these drugs on a daily basis over the previous year. Furthermore, a minimum of seven per cent of last-year users of any drug type were taking drugs on a weekly or more frequent basis over the preceding twelve months. This indicates that a sizeable minority of 'last-year users' are taking drugs frequently and regularly. However, the very small numbers in the survey reporting use of drugs such as crack (19 people), heroin (23 people) or Methadone (9 people) should also be noted. It is also arguable whether monthly use of certain Class A drugs, such as mushrooms, could be construed as dependent or problematic. We would stress again, then, that the measure of monthly use should only be viewed as a rough and indirect indicator of risk.

In addition, vulnerable groups were more likely to be involved in anti-social, drug-related behaviours such as perpetrating crimes to buy drugs and selling drugs to others (see Table 1.2). Here, a third of those who had ever slept rough admitted ever selling drugs and one in five serial runaways reported carrying out some kind of criminal activity in order to obtain drugs. These categories of vunerable group are defined in more detail later, in the relevant chapters.

Table 1.2: *Percentage of respondents reporting different drug-related behaviour and offending*

Has respondent:	Sold drugs	Committed a crime to buy drugs	Fought under influence of drugs	Stolen under the influence of drugs	A closest friend who uses drugs
School truants & excludees (aged 12 to 16)					
Truants	18	9	11	4	35
Excludees	20	12	18	5	31
Attenders	3	1	8	0	10
Offenders (aged 12 to 30)					
Serious/persistent offenders	21	10	19	10	53
Minor offenders	13	1	6	2	44
Non-offenders	5	1	3	1	18
Homeless young people (aged 16 to 30) & runaways (aged 12 to 30)					
Rough sleepers	34	23	19	5	58
Non-rough sleeping homeless	6	4	8	3	33
Never homeless	8	2	6	3	27
Serial runaways	30	20	22	16	53
One-off runaways	8	4	13	4	34
Never runaway	7	1	5	2	22
Those with drug-using parents & siblings (aged 12 to 30)					
Parent ever used drugs	17	3	6	4	29
Parent never used drugs	7	4	9	4	19
Older sibling ever used drugs	23	4	11	0	36
Older sibling never used drugs	5	0	24	0	6
Unweighted (n) in total sample	*1,896*	*1,909*	*1,164*	*1,164*	*4,360*

Source: YLS weighted data. Only those respondents who reported ever taking drugs (other than solvents) were asked if they had ever (1) sold drugs to someone else or (2) committed a crime to get the money to buy drugs. Only respondents who took drugs in the last year were asked whether they had (1) got into a fight or (2) stolen something whilst under the influence of drugs. All respondents were asked whether their closest friend took (unprescribed) drugs. Total unweighted sample sizes for vulnerable groups can be found in the tables in subsequent relevant chapters.

Nonetheless, we should also consider the overlaps between vulnerable groups to assess how far these characteristics may be related, and perhaps caused by similar events and situations. Table 1.3 shows the correlations in membership of some of the vulnerable groups considered in this report, across the full 12 to 30 age group. A strong correlation would have a coefficient close to one or, for variables with weaker correlations, closer to zero. In this case, the coefficients were not that large, indicating that there may be independent social processes involving different forms of vulnerability to drug use in operation among these young people.

However, all the associations were positive and a large number of the correlations were statistically significant. Frequency of offending, however, did not appear to have a strong relationship with all other vulnerable groups, which is perhaps surprising. It may be that there are degrees of problems with circumstances at home and at school that are distinct from more severe forms of delinquency represented by persistent offending. Those with parents who use drugs (on a lifetime basis) did not appear to have strong associations with any of the other vulnerable groups.

Table 1.3:	Correlations in membership of vulnerable groups (aged 12 to 30)		
	Frequency of truanting when at school	Frequency of offending in lifetime	Frequency of running away from home
Frequency of offending in lifetime	***0.24		
Frequency of running away from home	***0.23	***0.10	
Parent used any drug in their lifetime	0.04	**0.10	*0.05

Source: YLS and BCS weighted data. * $p<0.05$; ** $p<0.01$; *** $p<0.001$ using Kendall's tau-b (a measure of the association between rank orders, taking ties into account). 'Frequency of truanting' is measured on an ordinal scale: more than three days a week, two to three days a week, one day a week, two to three days a month, one day a month, one day a term, less than one day a term and never. 'Frequency of offending' is the total number of lifetime offences reported by the respondent. 'Frequency of running away from home' is the total number of times the respondent reported running away from home before the age of 16.

The information presented from the YLS provides baseline data on the prevalence of drug use among both young people in general and certain vulnerable groups. It also gives at least some indication of levels of use that border on the problematic. Given the methodological limitations (for instance, that issues around the development of drug use are best assessed through longitudinal research), this report is cautious over providing any general assessment of factors connecting drug use and vulnerability. We recognise that there are a host of features involving the family, the environment (including social deprivation and exclusion), peer influences, drug access/availability and health and criminological correlates that act within a "web of causation" (Lloyd, 1998: p.227). We do not therefore suggest that there is necessarily any causal link between truanting or offending and drug use. Being in a vulnerable group and using drugs may both be related to other factors and be interconnected in ways that reinforce each other.

This report concentrates on providing a range of basic insights into the extent and nature of drug use among specific groups of young people who are currently of considerable interest to policy makers and researchers. Firstly, Chapter two presents findings on the prevalence of and ease of access to drugs among school age children, comparing rates between truants, excludees and those who regularly attend school. Young offenders are discussed in Chapter three, which includes analyses of serious and/or persistent offenders, minor offenders and those who claim to have never broken the law. Substance use among those who have ever experienced homelessness is described in Chapter four and this incorporates data on those who have run away from home at some point in their lives. Chapter five presents data on the levels of drug use within families and households, focusing on young people with drug-using parents and siblings. Chapter six summarises the important findings in the light of emerging themes and briefly offers some implications for policy makers and future research.

2   School truants and excludees

Introduction

Studies of school-age drug use have traditionally centred on surveys in a classroom setting (e.g. Balding, 2000; Goddard and Higgins, 1999 & 2000; Wright and Pearl, 2000). Some of these school surveys have suggested a decline in the levels of drug use in recent years from a peak in the mid-1990s (Plant and Miller, 2000; Balding, 2000). However, little UK research has been undertaken examining patterns or trends of drug use among truant and excluded populations, although it has been recognised that expulsion and exclusion from school are very strong predictors of problem drug use (Lloyd, 1998; Miller and Plant, 1999).

It has been estimated that every year at least one million young people truant, 13,000 are permanently excluded and over 100,000 temporarily excluded from school (SEU, 1998a). Graham and Bowling (1995) indicate, in their analysis of the 1992/93 YLS data, that temporary and permanent school exclusion are closely associated with offending. Thus, it seems that, as the Social Exclusion Unit suggests, excluded pupils are at a greater risk of becoming involved in crime and other illicit behaviours.

It was possible within the YLS to extract a sample of those young people aged between 12 and 16 who truanted or were excluded from school to set against those who regularly attended. The YLS asked respondents whether they had truanted from school for a whole day in the past school year without permission. Within this sample of at least occasional truants, the sexes were equally represented, their mean age was 15 years and 93 per cent of them were white.

Similarly, it was possible to derive a sample of young people (aged between 12 and 16) who were 'excluded' from school on a potentially regular basis. The definition of 'excluded' includes those who missed school at least one day per term (more regular truancy) or had been expelled or suspended at some point during their school career. In this sample, almost three-quarters were male, the mean age was 14 years, and 90 per cent were white.

Pupils were defined as 'school attenders' if they reported going to school on a consistent basis, that is, they were neither truants nor excludees. School attenders in the YLS sample had equal gender representation, a mean age of 14 years and were 90 per cent white.

Levels of overlap should be noted: 45 per cent of the relatively small group of excludees were also in the truant sample. This method was chosen to shed some light on the degrees of vulnerability among young people of school age as well as offering some comparison with categories used in the main YLS report (Flood-Page *et al.*, 2000).

Table 2.1 compares lifetime and last year drug use across these three categories. It shows that truants and excludees tended to have markedly higher rates of drug use than school attenders. The YLS found that half of truants and excludees had taken at least one drug in their lives. This level was four times higher than for regular school attenders. It should be noted that the proportion using any drug in the last year can be lower than the percentage using individual drugs. This is because only those with invalid answers to ALL questions on last year use (i.e. "not asked", "don't want to answer" or "missing") were excluded from the 'any drug' category (4 people overall). The numbers with these invalid responses for individual drug types over the last year were often more than this.

There were high degrees of polydrug use among truants and school excludees, with cannabis, solvents, poppers (amyl nitrite) and amphetamine featuring strongly. Levels of heroin use – negligible among school attenders – were two per cent for truants and excludees on a lifetime basis. The level of consumption of any Class A drug once a month during the last year was significantly higher for excludees than for those who routinely attended school. Other research into drug use by school-aged young people highlights a similar pattern of experimentation, with cannabis use most prominent, followed by use of amphetamine, solvents, magic mushrooms and poppers. Progression to heroin or cocaine use is rare and usually occurs later in a young person's drug-using career (Aldridge *et al.*, 1999; Goddard and Higgins, 2000).

Table 2.1: *Percentage of truants, excludees and attenders using drugs in their lifetime and the last year (aged 12 to 16)*

	Lifetime			Last Year		
	Truants	Excludees	Attenders	Truants	Excludees	Attenders
Amphetamine	***15	***12	2	***10	***8	1
Cannabis	***50	***42	10	***42	***34	8
Cocaine	***5	**3	-	**2	*3	-
Crack	0	*2	-	0	**2	0
Ecstasy	***4	***7	-	**2	***5	-
Heroin	**2	**2	-	0	**2	0
LSD	***8	***8	-	***4	***7	-
Mushrooms	***9	***11	1	***5	***8	-
Methadone	1	**2	-	0	*2	0
Poppers	***11	***16	2	***6	***12	1
Solvents	***21	***18	4	***9	***13	2
Steroids	**3	**4	-	0	*2	-
Tranquillisers	***6	***9	-	***4	***8	-
Monthly Class A	NA	NA	NA	-	**7	0
Any drug	***54	***50	13	***42	***36	9
Unweighted (n)	*193*	*135*	*1,206*	*187*	*129*	*1,188*

Source: YLS weighted data. * $p<0.05$; ** $p<0.01$; *** $p<0.001$ using Pearson's χ^2 or Fisher's Exact Test where appropriate, performed on 'truants' and 'excludees' versus 'attenders'. '-' = less than 0.5%. 'Monthly Class A' is defined as 'use of any Class A drug at least once a month in the last year'. NA = not applicable (as monthly use is over the last year).

If we compare the prevalence of drug use in the school-attending sub-population with recent school surveys, a similar pattern emerges. The National Statistics study of smoking, drinking and drug use within schools (Goddard and Higgins, 1999) indicated a lifetime prevalence rate of 13 per cent among boys and girls aged between 11 and 15 years. This compares closely with a lifetime prevalence rate of 15 per cent among the 12- to 16-year-olds sampled in the YLS. The YLS lifetime and last-year prevalence rates for truants and excludees were not as high as those for school excludees in a number of Pupil Referral Units (PRU) across North West London, where the last month rate was 58 per cent (Powis *et al.*, 1998). However, this high figure may reflect the deprived, inner-city area from where the PRU attenders were drawn. There were other important factors: the PRU sample was older (14 to 16) than the YLS sample (12 to 16) and included only pupils from the lower academic streams.

Gender

School-based studies have tended to suggest that young males have somewhat higher levels of experimentation with drugs than young females (Goddard and Higgins, 1999; Balding, 2000). However, in a recent longitudinal study of young people in two North of England regions, drug use levels were the same for 15 to 16 year old males and females (Aldridge et al., 1999). Tables 2.2 and 2.3 below show the gender differences in the YLS between regular school attenders, truants and those excluded from school. Among the attenders, males had fractionally higher prevalence rates than females (not statistically significant), both on a lifetime and a last-year basis. However, female truants and excludees tended to have considerably higher prevalence rates than their male counterparts for most drugs.

Table 2.2: **Percentage of truants, excludees and attenders using drugs in their lifetime by sex (aged 12 to 16)**

	Truants		Excludees		Attenders	
	Male	Female	Male	Female	Male	Female
Amphetamine	12	19	*8	26	3	2
Cannabis	*43	58	39	53	11	8
Cocaine	7	3	4	0	0	1
Crack	0	0	2	0	-	0
Ecstasy	3	4	8	3	-	-
Heroin	2	1	3	0	0	-
LSD	5	11	*4	19	1	-
Mushrooms	8	10	8	19	1	-
Methadone	0	1	2	3	-	-
Poppers	9	13	14	23	2	2
Solvents	**12	29	**13	35	4	3
Steroids	2	3	4	0	*1	0
Tranquillisers	**1	12	*5	19	1	1
Any drug	*45	63	*45	67	15	12
Unweighted (n)	105	88	102	33	576	630

Source: YLS weighted data. * $p<0.05$; ** $p<0.01$; *** $p<0.001$ using Pearson's χ^2 or Fisher's Exact Test where appropriate, performed on 'males' versus 'females' for the 'truants', 'excludees' and 'attenders'. '-' = less than 0.5%.

Although lifetime prevalence rates among the regular school attenders were slightly higher for young males, in the truant and excluded samples, females tended to report considerably higher levels of drug use. Roughly, two-thirds of female excludees reported lifetime use of any drug, and almost as many female truants, as opposed to less than half of their male equivalents. Numbers of females in the excluded category particularly were rather small (33 people), and conclusions must therefore remain tentative. Young female truants and excludees were significantly more likely to report lifetime use of solvents and tranquillisers than their male equivalents. Young female school excludees also reported significantly higher lifetime use of LSD and amphetamine, whilst cannabis use was significantly higher for female truants than for their male counterparts. Nevertheless, despite these higher lifetime rates for use of 'recreational' drugs among young women, the rates for more harmful drugs such as heroin, cocaine and crack were not statistically significantly different.

Table 2.3: Percentage of truants, excludees and attenders using drugs in the last year by sex (aged 12 to 16)

	Truants		Excludees		Attenders	
	Male	Female	Male	Female	Male	Female
Amphetamine	7	14	*4	17	1	1
Cannabis	**32	52	*29	52	9	7
Cocaine	2	3	3	0	0	1
Crack	0	0	2	0	0	0
Ecstasy	3	2	5	3	-	0
Heroin	0	0	2	0	0	0
LSD	*1	8	**2	20	-	-
Mushrooms	3	6	*4	17	1	-
Methadone	0	0	2	0	0	0
Tranquillisers	**0	9	*4	17	0	-
Poppers	4	8	9	21	1	1
Steroids	0	0	2	0	-	0
Solvents	5	11	*8	27	2	1
Any drug	**32	52	**29	57	10	9
Monthly Class A	-	-	*3	17	0	0
Unweighted (n)	101	86	98	31	562	626

Source: YLS weighted data. * $p<0.05$; ** $p<0.01$; *** $p<0.001$ using Pearson's χ^2 or Fisher's Exact Test where appropriate, performed on 'males' versus 'females' for the 'truants', 'excludees' and 'attenders'. '-' = less than 0.5%. 'Monthly Class A' is defined as 'use of any Class A drug once a month in the last year'.

Last-year drug use is presented in Table 2.3 and shows a similar pattern to lifetime prevalence among male and female school-age young people. Among the school-attending sample, there was near parity, with slightly higher last-year rates generally reported by males. This situation was strikingly reversed in the truant and excluded samples. Here, use of any drug among females who were excluded from school was nearly twice that of their male counterparts; it was also much higher for females in the truant sample (both differences were significant). These figures show nearly half of all female truants and excludees reporting consumption of cannabis in the last year. Female truants were significantly more likely than their male counterparts to report taking cannabis, LSD and tranquillisers in the last year. Female excludees reported significantly higher levels of amphetamine, cannabis, LSD, magic mushroom, tranquilliser and solvent use in the last year. Female truants and excludees were also significantly more likely than males to report monthly Class A drug use during the previous year, although no attenders of either sex reported doing so.

Further research could be usefully carried out on the subject of initiation into drug use by truants and excludees. Overall, initiation into drug use did not differ between females and males, with a mean age of first use of any drug of 16 years (see Flood-Page *et al.*, 2000). However, due to the relatively small sample sizes and individual question response rates, the concept of 'age of first use by vulnerable group' unfortunately cannot be explored in detail for specific drugs.

Access

The following section attempts to explore the levels of access to drugs among different school-aged sub-groups. One of the Government's key objectives is to "stifle the availability of illegal drugs on our streets" and specifically "to reduce access to all drugs among young people (under 25) significantly" (UKADCU, 2000). The ease of access to particular drugs may help explain prevalence rates for different vulnerable groups as well as providing a baseline indicator from which to track the success or failure of the anti-drugs strategy in reaching these groups and affecting supply. The levels of exposure to pre-existing drug-using groups and the degree of access to drug markets have been identified as major factors in determining rates of drug use among vulnerable groups (Lloyd, 1998).

YLS respondents were asked how easy it would be to get hold of a range of drugs (cannabis, amphetamine, cocaine, ecstasy, mushrooms and heroin) if they wanted to and had the time and money to do so. The potential responses were: very or fairly easy or difficult, 'it varies' and 'do not know'. Self-reported access rates (for those who stated that access was 'very' or 'fairly' easy versus those finding access difficult, variable or unknown) for the six drugs about which questions were asked are presented below in Table 2.4 by sex.

Table 2.4:   **Percentage of truants, excludees and attenders finding it 'easy' to obtain selected drugs by sex (aged 12 to 16)**

	Truants		Excludees		Attenders	
	Male	Female	Male	Female	Male	Female
Amphetamine	**41	60	37	43	29	29
Cannabis	*53	69	55	65	33	29
Cocaine	**17	35	21	26	*12	16
Ecstasy	*21	47	**21	45	17	18
Heroin	17	27	21	29	10	12
Mushrooms	*21	36	24	29	13	16
Unweighted (n)	105	88	102	33	639	640

Source: YLS weighted data. * $p<0.05$; ** $p<0.01$; *** $p<0.001$ using Pearson's χ^2 Test, performed on 'males' versus 'females' for the 'truants', 'excludees' and 'attenders'.

Female excludees and particularly truants were generally more likely to report finding it easier to get drugs than equivalent males. For school attenders, the picture was more complicated, as access to cannabis was perceived to be easier by males than by females and equal for amphetamine. For the other drugs, including heroin and cocaine (the latter significantly so), a greater proportion of females thought that access was very or fairly easy. It has been suggested that younger females' relative ease in obtaining drugs in comparison with young males may be due to the influence of older boyfriends with well-established drug-taking habits (Aldridge et al., 1999).

Discussion

Our sample of young people aged between 12 and 16 years indicates higher lifetime and last-year prevalence rates for truants and for those who are temporarily or permanently excluded from school in comparison with those who routinely attend school. Given the size of these populations nationally, this would suggest that current school-based surveys might produce modest underestimates of school-age drug use. Further in-depth studies of truants and school excludees are required to determine the exact extent and nature of drug use in these groups and to illuminate their initiation into drug use. Such research may also provide greater insights into the relative risks for different school-aged vulnerable groups in terms of early initiation and the influences of peer networks.

Our analysis suggests that the prevalence of drug use is generally much higher for female truants and excludees in comparison to males. One should qualify this statement by acknowledging some differences in the prevalence rates for different types of drugs (for example, greater use of more harmful drugs such as heroin and crack by male excludees). There were significant differences between male and female truants and those excluded from school. This finding points to females aged between 12 and 16, who truant from or are excluded from school, being at greater risk of exposure to drug use than their male counterparts (and may in fact be the reason why they are excluded). Drugs prevention should consider targeting young excludees and truants to determine which interventions are appropriate for them, and particularly whether specific strategies are required for female non-attenders. Although the current analyses are unable to resolve whether this higher prevalence of drug use leads to dependent use, comparatively heavy drug use at a younger age is often a sign of greater problems later. Whilst young female excludees have higher levels of Class A drug use within the last month in comparison with young males, numbers of such regular users are small. More detailed surveillance of drug use in this population, tracking their behaviour as they grow older, is recommended.

3   Young offenders

Introduction

The links between criminal offending and drug use are well established (for a summary see Goulden *et al.*, forthcoming; Hough, 1996; Newburn, 1998). Some aetiological explanations of drug use and offending suggest that they may develop in parallel, with involvement in crime (especially acquisitive crime) predating drug use, where both eventually come to sustain each other (Edmunds *et al.*, 1999). However, these connections remain subject to debate, given the lack of longitudinal research involving those prone to serious offending and drug use.

Existing research has focused upon drug use and criminal behaviour among criminal justice populations (Edmunds *et al.*, 1998; Bennett, 1998 & 2000) or within drug treatment settings (Gossop *et al.*, 1998). An alternative measure of the linkages between offending and drug use can be explored through the YLS.

The YLS provides additional contextual information on the extent and nature of drug use among the general population, including offenders who had not engaged with the criminal justice system. It was possible to derive a typology of offenders based upon the seriousness of offences reported to the YLS (it is worth emphasising that this is dependent on self-reported offending, with all the caveats that entails). The full sample of those aged between 12 and 30 years was used. Ideally, a younger cohort would have been chosen, but small sample sizes prohibited this approach.

- 'Serious and/or persistent offenders' are defined as those who admitted three or more minor offences in the last year and/or at least one serious offence. Hence, it is also a measure of relatively recent offending behaviour. These serious offences include stealing a car or motor-bike, burglary, snatch theft, pick-pocketing, threatening someone to get money or possessions, assault and injuring someone with a weapon. These serious and/or persistent offenders were 74 per cent male and 94 per cent white with a mean age of 19 years (296 people).
- 'Minor offenders' are defined as those who reported committing one or two minor offences in the last year (for example, fraud or shoplifting). They were 64 per cent male and 93 per cent white with a mean age of 21 years (228 people).

- The 'non-offenders' group is defined as those young people who reported never committing any offence. They were 40 per cent male and 91 per cent white, with a mean age of 20 years (2,112 people). Offenders who reported offending but not within the last year were excluded from the analyses in this chapter.

The groupings have been chosen to be consistent with the main YLS report (Flood-Page *et al.*, 2000) and to allow some estimation of degree in relation to the drug-crime nexus. Table 3.1 shows the prevalence rates of drug use among serious, minor and non-offenders.

Table 3.1: *Percentage of serious/persistent, minor and non-offenders using drugs in their lifetime and the last year (aged 12 to 30)*

| | Lifetime | | | Last Year | | |
	Serious/ Persistent	Minor offender	Non- offender	Serious/ Persistent	Minor offender	Non- offender
Amphetamine	***42	***36	9	***24	***17	3
Cannabis	***70	***59	24	***56	***44	13
Cocaine	***21	***17	2	***13	***12	1
Crack	***5	***2	-	***2	0	0
Ecstasy	***19	***17	4	***12	***8	1
Heroin	***6	***3	-	***3	0	0
LSD	***25	***17	4	***8	***4	-
Mushrooms	***19	***19	4	***6	***7	-
Methadone	***3	***2	-	***2	0	0
Poppers	***34	***33	7	***11	***8	1
Solvents	***26	***18	2	***7	***3	-
Steroids	***4	***2	-	**2	-	-
Tranquillisers	***15	***7	1	***5	*2	-
Any drug	***74	***67	26	***58	***49	14
Monthly Class A	NA	NA	NA	***7	***3	-
Unweighted (n)	296	228	2,112	296	228	2,112

Source: YLS weighted data. * $p<0.05$; ** $p<0.01$; *** $p<0.001$ using Pearson's χ^2 or Fisher's Exact Test, where appropriate, performed on 'serious &/or persistent offenders' and 'minor offenders' versus 'non-offenders'. '-' = less than 0.5%. 'Monthly Class A' is defined as 'use of any Class A drug at least once a month in the last year'. NA = not applicable (as monthly use is over the last year).

Three-quarters of serious and/or persistent offenders and two-thirds of minor offenders reported ever using drugs. For non-offenders, the equivalent figure was one in four. For the last year, about half of all offenders, but only one in seven non-offenders used an illicit drug. The differences in prevalence rates between the offender populations and non-offenders were strongly statistically significant and there was a clearer relationship between rate and type of offending and drug use, with serious and persistent offenders having the highest prevalence rates and non-offenders the lowest. Both serious and minor offenders were likely to have used a variety of drugs, with particularly widespread use of cannabis (70% lifetime use among serious offenders), amphetamine and poppers. Reported use of the more harmful drugs such as heroin, cocaine and crack was also much higher in these samples than in the non-offender group.

Gender

Table 3.2 shows the gender differentials in lifetime drug use among offender and non-offender populations. Reasonably close parity in prevalence rates between sexes can be seen within both the non-offender and minor offender samples. However, female minor offenders reported nearly twice the level of solvent use in comparison with their male counterparts, for instance.

Table 3.2: *Percentage of serious/persistent, minor and non-offenders using drugs in their lifetime (aged 12 to 30)*

	Serious &/or persistent offenders		Minor offenders		Non-offenders	
	Male	Female	Male	Female	Male	Female
Amphetamine	45	34	36	37	10	9
Cannabis	72	67	61	56	24	24
Cocaine	**24	11	16	18	**3	2
Crack	6	3	4	0	-	-
Ecstasy	***23	8	19	15	4	4
Heroin	6	4	2	5	-	-
LSD	**28	14	20	11	4	5
Mushrooms	**23	8	**24	10	***6	3
Methadone	3	2	2	4	0	-
Poppers	**38	22	34	31	8	7
Solvents	26	25	*13	25	1	2
Steroids	*5	0	4	0	1	-
Tranquillisers	**18	7	9	5	1	1
Any drug	*77	66	67	66	26	26
Unweighted (n)	*213*	*83*	*134*	*93*	*801*	*1,311*

Source: YLS weighted data. * $p<0.05$; ** $p<0.01$; *** $p<0.001$ using Pearson's χ^2 or Fisher's Exact Test, where appropriate, performed on 'males' versus 'females' for 'serious &/or persistent offenders', 'minor offenders' and 'non-offenders'. '-' = less than 0.5%.

Among the serious and/or persistent offenders, young males had much higher levels of drug use. This was true for all drug categories, with statistically significant differences noticeable for cocaine, ecstasy, LSD, mushrooms, tranquillisers, poppers, steroids and solvents. By way of comparison with lifetime prevalence rates, levels of drug use in the last year are presented below in Table 3.3.

Table 3.3: **Percentage of serious/persistent, minor and non-offenders using drugs in the last year (aged 12 to 30)**

	Serious &/or persistent offenders		Minor offenders		Non-offenders	
	Male	Female	Male	Female	Male	Female
Amphetamine	26	19	19	13	3	3
Cannabis	56	57	45	42	13	13
Cocaine	14	8	13	10	2	1
Crack	3	1	0	0	0	0
Ecstasy	***16	3	8	8	1	1
Heroin	4	1	0	0	0	0
LSD	10	4	4	4	-	-
Mushrooms	*7	1	*10	3	1	-
Methadone	2	1	0	0	0	0
Tranquillisers	6	4	2	2	-	-
Poppers	*13	4	8	6	2	1
Steroids	2	0	1	0	-	0
Solvents	8	5	**1	8	0	-
Any drug	59	54	48	51	14	14
Monthly Class A	*9	2	3	4	1	-
Unweighted (n)	226	80	152	84	827	1,235

Source: YLS weighted data. * p<0.05; ** p<0.01; *** p<0.001 using Pearson's χ^2 or Fisher's Exact Test, where appropriate, performed on 'males' versus 'females' for 'serious &/or persistent offenders', 'minor offenders' and 'non-offenders'. '-' = less than 0.5%. 'Monthly Class A' is defined as 'use of any Class A drug at least once a month in the last year'.

Prevalence of drug use in the last year by sex among minor offenders and non-offenders was reasonably similar, with male minor offenders more likely to report use of mushrooms and female minor offenders more likely to use solvents in the last year. Patterns of drug use among serious and/or persistent offenders showed higher rates reported by males in all categories with statistically significant differences noticeable in use of ecstasy, mushrooms and poppers.

Further analysis of the YLS suggests that drug use in the last year was strongly associated with offending among 12- to 17-year-old males, as was use in the last month for 18- to 30-year-old males (see Flood-Page *et al.*, 2000). Over half of all serious offenders, male and female, reported using cannabis in the last year compared with only 13 per cent of male and female non-offenders.

Discussion

The levels of lifetime and last-year drug use were closely associated with offender type, with 74 per cent of serious and/or persistent offenders reporting lifetime use, and 57 per cent stating that they used drugs in the last year. Offenders were more likely to use or have tried a range of drugs in comparison with non-offenders. The analysis shows that those who committed offences of a more serious nature were more likely to use drugs with greater regularity, particularly men.

The data do not indicate how far drug use was experimental or problematic and the results should be treated with a degree of caution. Further research is required to supplement these basic prevalence data to determine the extent of dependent use in offending and non-offending populations of young people. Moreover, the data presented above are unable to demonstrate causal associations between drug use and different types of crime. For example, we are unable to say what proportion of crime can be attributed to the use of and desire for drugs. However, the data presented are unique in that these offenders do not necessarily have extensive involvement with the criminal justice system and remain at large at the time of the survey. By including those offenders who have not been to court, arrested by the police or incarcerated within prison, one could argue that the data provide a more balanced picture of drug-using patterns among offenders in general.

On the other hand, prolific offenders (liable to be caught and imprisoned or less likely to co-operate with surveys of offending behaviour and drug use) might be under-represented. This can be illustrated with reference to data collected from those interviewed and urine tested for drugs whilst being held on arrest in police custody suites (Bennett, 2000). For the sample of arrestees aged between 17 and 24, this research suggests much higher levels of drug use than those found in the YLS. For example, rates of last-year use of heroin, crack and cocaine all stood at around 20 per cent among arrestees, compared with a range of one to eight per cent for male and female serious and/or persistent offenders in the YLS.

4   Homeless young people and runaways

Homeless young people

Introduction

Homelessness exists on a continuum. It can vary from 'rooflessness' or sleeping rough, to living in bed and breakfast accommodation and hostels, to an "inability to leave unsatisfactory housing conditions" (Rugg, 2000: p.5). Young people's experience of accommodation can be fairly volatile after first leaving home, but this instability can easily gradate into more problematic situations and even homelessness – particularly for certain susceptible groups. Homeless young people are also prone to complicating and inter-related problems such as mental and physical illnesses, learning difficulties, disablement, offending and substance dependence (Wade and Barnett, 1999). Rates of drug use can be very high among the young homeless and drug-related problems within this group may predate (Desai *et al.*, 2000), be amplified by or directly result from episodes of homelessness. However, only nine per cent of a sample of 340 single homeless people in Sheffield admitted a history of drug abuse (Shanks *et al.*, 1994). This compares with other studies where recorded levels of lifetime use of any drug were as high as 76 per cent (Carlen, 1996: p.130) and 88 per cent (Flemen, 1997).

For instance, a recent case-control study of 160 homeless London youth, aged 16 to 21, concluded that "... childhood experiences, educational attainment and the prior presence of psychiatric disorder all independently increase the likelihood of homelessness..." (Craig and Hodson, 1998: p.1379). Two-thirds of this group were followed up at one year, when persistent substance use was found to be critical in thwarting resettlement attempts and related to more serious offending and antisocial behaviour (Craig and Hodson, 2000). The cumulative length of time spent homeless may also be associated with an increasing risk of substance abuse (Kipke *et al.*, 1997). Homeless young people may use drugs for the same reasons as other young people, although the short-term 'therapeutic' aspects may be more important. Drugs can also provide "... (for some, at least) a rationale for getting up in the mornings, an occupational framework to the day, and a sense of community and identification with other drug users" (Carlen, 1996: p.131).

Homeless young people in the YLS

The YLS asked whether the respondent had ever been homeless, for a period of one month or longer. Respondents, who stated they had, were also asked if they had experienced a period of sleeping rough and if so, for how long. The first part of the question thus relies upon the respondents' own subjective definition of homelessness, which can be just as important as more objective criteria (ibid.: pp.24–26). Although these questions only relate to past episodes of homelessness (the YLS being a household survey), they nevertheless remain valuable indicators of vulnerability to drug misuse. This is particularly true as contacts with homeless people are likely to underestimate the total population by perhaps two-thirds (Fisher *et al.*, 1994) and, consequently, research into this hard-to-reach group of young people is rare.

Nearly four per cent of the YLS sample aged 16 to 30 (156 people) stated that they had been homeless for more than one month at some point in their lives and just over one per cent had slept rough. This translates into a figure for England and Wales of 120,000 young people (aged 16 to 30 at the time of the survey) having ever slept rough. 'Sleeping rough' was defined in the YLS as "sleeping on the streets or some other unsheltered public place, e.g. park, field, etc.".

The minimum current age of anyone who had been homeless in the YLS was 16, so the results presented here are restricted to 16- to 30-year-olds. Approximately half of the rough sleepers had been on the streets for a month or longer but only one in ten (one in a thousand of the whole sample) for more than six months. It is hard to draw exact comparisons, but a report by the Social Exclusion Unit (1998b) states that some 12,400 people, of all ages, drift in and out of sleeping rough in England over the course of a year. Another study estimates, albeit with fairly wide definitions, the total number of homeless young people aged 16 to 24 to be around a quarter of a million (Evans, 1996), a third of whom may be 18 or under (Adamczuk, 2000).

In the YLS, females were more likely than males to have experienced homelessness by a ratio of three to two. This may be because males who become homeless or runaway are less likely to return to the family home and so will not be captured in a household survey. However, other studies have also discovered an increasing over-representation of females particularly among the young homeless (Rugg, 2000: p.5). The vast majority of the YLS homeless group was white (92%) and over 24 years of age (64%). It should also be remembered that the episode(s) of homelessness could have occurred at any time during the respondent's life. This does, however, highlight the fluid nature of homelessness, and that it is not necessarily an irrevocable state of existence. It may mean also that YLS respondents have had less severely problematic drug use than those who have remained homeless or sleeping rough.

Drug use

Differences in drug use between those who had and had not experienced homelessness were apparent though not substantial, as can be seen from Table 4.1, but rates among those who had ever slept rough were very high. For these young people, lifetime use of the more harmful drugs (i.e. heroin, cocaine and crack), tranquillisers, steroids, solvents and hallucinogens (i.e. LSD and mushrooms) was four to ten times higher, than for the 'never been homeless'. The sample size for rough sleepers was small (38 people), but differences remained statistically significant when compared with both the never homeless and the non-rough sleeping homeless. The latter group had similar rates of lifetime use to the never homeless, except for hallucinogens and amphetamine, where differences were strongly significant.

Contrasts in more recent use were less stark, which perhaps suggests that some respondents had previously experienced a chaotic phase in their lives, involving a temporary but extended period of homelessness combined with increased use of drugs. There is no evidence, however, that these events were coterminous. Nonetheless, those who had ever slept rough continued to have higher last year usage of a range of drugs, including cocaine, and a tenth were still using a Class A drug at least once a month. Differences between the non-rough sleeping homeless and the never homeless diminished greatly at the last-year level, although there remained 50 per cent more cannabis use among the non-rough sleeping homeless.

Table 4.1: **Percentage of those ever homeless using drugs in their lifetime and the last year (aged 12 to 30)**

	Lifetime drug use			Last year drug use		
	Homeless rough sleeper	Homeless non rough sleeper	Never been homeless	Homeless rough sleeper	Homeless non rough sleeper	Never been homeless
Amphetamine	***65	**38	26	***39	10	11
Cannabis	**72	*62	49	**54	*43	30
Cocaine	***40	8	10	**18	6	6
Crack	***15	3	2	3	1	-
Ecstasy	***36	18	13	*15	6	6
Heroin	**10	2	2	*5	1	1
LSD	***62	***33	14	5	1	2
Mushrooms	***63	***28	12	*11	1	3
Methadone	*5	0	1	0	0	-
Poppers	***50	*29	20	*13	5	4
Solvents	***43	14	8	3	0	1
Steroids	*8	2	1	0	1	1
Tranquillisers	***38	7	4	**10	0	1
Monthly Class A	NA	NA	NA	*10	2	3
Any drug	***80	*65	53	**53	*45	32
Unweighted (n)	38	118	3,396	36	110	3,330

Source: YLS weighted data. * $p<0.05$; ** $p<0.01$; *** $p<0.001$ using Pearson's χ^2 or Fisher's Exact Test where appropriate, performed on 'rough sleepers' and 'non-rough sleeping homeless' versus 'never homeless'. '-' = less than 0.5%. 'Monthly Class A' is defined as use of any Class A drug once a month in the last year. NA = not applicable (as monthly use is over the last year).

With only limited numbers in the YLS reporting homelessness, particularly any sleeping rough, separate examination of males and females is difficult. The analyses according to sex, presented in Table 4.2, should therefore be handled with care, and the homeless groups have been recombined to increase the sample size. There nevertheless appeared to be considerable contrasts in drug use remaining after controlling for sex, although there were no significant differences in monthly use of Class A drugs. For instance, lifetime use of all substances bar Methadone was statistically significantly higher for homeless compared to never homeless males. Use of the more harmful drugs was especially pronounced, with nine per cent of homeless males having ever used heroin, 15 per cent crack and 28 per cent cocaine. Other drugs ever used by the greater part of homeless males were cannabis, amphetamine and hallucinogens.

Differences in lifetime use between males and females within the homeless group were less severe. Even so, the variations in use, particularly of hallucinogens but also cocaine, crack, cannabis and steroids, were all statistically significant at $p<0.05$ (the results of significance tests for differences between males and females are not shown in Table 4.2). Among females, there was a weaker but perceptible relationship between ever being homeless and using drugs. Statistically significant differences were confined to drugs other than opiates or cocaine, with rates generally two to three times higher across the female homeless group.

Table 4.2: **Percentage of those ever homeless using drugs in their lifetime and the last year by sex (aged 16 to 30)**

| | Lifetime | | | | Last Year | | | |
| | Males | | Females | | Males | | Females | |
	H	NH	H	NH	H	NH	H	NH
Amphetamine	***56	31	***40	21	24	13	*16	8
Cannabis	**77	55	*57	42	***63	36	34	23
Cocaine	**28	14	11	6	16	8	4	3
Crack	***15	3	3	1	2	1	1	-
Ecstasy	**33	18	**17	8	14	9	6	3
Heroin	*9	2	1	1	*6	1	0	-
LSD	***62	19	***29	10	6	3	1	1
Mushrooms	***58	17	***24	6	10	5	1	1
Methadone	2	1	1	-	0	1	0	-
Poppers	*42	26	***31	15	6	2	1	1
Solvents	**25	10	***20	6	8	6	*7	2
Steroids	*10	2	0	-	2	1	0	0
Tranquillisers	***28	6	*8	3	2	2	0	1
Any drug	**83	60	*61	46	***66	38	35	25
Monthly Class A	NA	NA	NA	NA	8	5	3	2
Unweighted (n)	51	1,568	105	1,828	48	1,533	98	1,797

Source: YLS weighted data. * $p<0.05$; ** $p<0.01$; *** $p<0.001$ using Pearson's χ^2 or Fisher's Exact Test where appropriate, performed on 'homeless' versus 'never homeless' groups for 'males' and 'females'. H = Ever homeless; NH = Never homeless; '-' = less than 0.5%. 'Monthly Class A' is defined as 'use of any Class A drug at least once a month in the last year'. NA = Not applicable (as monthly use is over the last year).

Runaways

Introduction

Childhood experience of running away from home can be a precursor to later periods of homelessness or sleeping rough (Heffron et al., 1997). Indeed, 'runaway' is often used as shorthand for youth homelessness (Wrate and Blair, 1999). One study estimated that 43,000 young people run away from home every year in Britain (a rate of six per 1,000 young people), while another, school-based population survey stated that one in seven young people aged under 16 had ever done so (Lawrenson, 1997). As with homelessness, there are important differences within this group of young people. Lawrenson (ibid.), for instance, categorises runaways into two groups, albeit with a degree of transition and overlap:

- One-off runaways: who do not travel far and generally go alone; are likely to come from poor backgrounds and reconstituted families and have a history of truanting.
- Serial runaways: have established patterns of running away, usually to escape abuse or rejection, with a danger of drifting into homelessness, prostitution or residential or substitutive care.

Lawrenson also states that rates of previous abuse and prostitution among runaways may be as high as 75 per cent and 20 per cent respectively. MacLeod (1997) reports that over a third of young homeless or runaway callers to ChildLine in the UK had fled home because of physical (27%) or sexual (8%) assault – these are probably underestimates. Similar findings can be seen from research conducted in the USA – almost half of a sample of 300 American runaway youths had a history of physical or sexual abuse (Stiffman, 1989), and this relationship was corroborated by Schaffner (1998) in a qualitative study of runaways in rural America. Furthermore, Schaffner interpreted running away as a last resort in escaping from abuse and not the 'impulsive decision' of an 'incorrigible delinquent'. Further qualitative work in the UK would be helpful in understanding the reasons why young people run away from their homes.

Runaways in the YLS

All YLS respondents were asked whether they had run away from home for one or more nights without telling their parents or guardians where they were. However, those aged over sixteen were only asked about incidents when they were younger – any incidents occurring at or over the age of sixteen were not recorded. Those answering in the affirmative were questioned further on the age they first ran away and the total number of times they had done so (again only in reference to when they were under sixteen). Respondents who were aged twelve to fifteen at the time of the survey were asked about all the times they had fled home.

The nature of the YLS as a household survey means that respondents probably under-represent the extreme forms of vulnerability, such as Lawrenson's 'serial runaways' outlined above. However, we were able to use the number of times the respondent reported running away to split the sub-sample into serial or multiple (i.e. reported running away more than once) and one-off (i.e. reported running away once) categories.

Almost six per cent of young people in the YLS had run away from home when less than sixteen years of age, and of these, one in seven had also experienced an episode of homelessness of a month or more. This compares with a rate of homelessness of only one in fifty for respondents who had never run away from home (this difference was statistically significant at $p<0.001$ using Pearson's χ^2 Test). It seems, therefore, that some of the factors behind youth homelessness may be common to those involved in running away – they are both likely to reflect reactions to difficulties with home circumstances. The Children's Society (1999), for instance, includes factors such as school problems, disagreements over lifestyle and personal issues (including drug and alcohol problems) and getting into trouble with the police, as potential spurs to running away from home. Hence, drug use may have been directly involved in periods of running away or homelessness and there is the potential that running away may reinforce existing use or lead on to new forms of use through peer influence.

Members of the 'runaways' group in the YLS were much younger in general than the 'homeless' group – almost half were under 21 at the time of interview, but again the vast majority were white (97%). As with the 'homeless' group, females appeared more likely to run away from home than males – 57 per cent of runaways in the YLS sample were girls (statistically significant at $p<0.05$ using Pearson's χ^2 Test).

Drug use

Again, there were clear patterns in lifetime drug use according to whether young people had run away from home before the age of sixteen (Table 4.3). There was a consistent relationship between drug use and the number of times a respondent had run away from home for both recall periods. Rates of lifetime use among the serial runaways were generally double to triple those of the one-offs and two to eight times the 'nevers'. The figures for serial runaways' lifetime use were particularly extreme for cocaine (23%), crack (8%), heroin (7%) and Methadone (5%), but all differences with the non-runaways were statistically significant at $p<0.001$, apart from steroids.

The contrasts remained for use of drugs in the previous year. This was striking as, for many of the respondents, incidents of running away may have occurred quite some time ago in their lives, but their drug use as a group remained higher than average. One in twenty-five serial runaways continued to use heroin, one in nine cocaine and one in three amphetamine. One in twelve were using Class A drugs at least monthly during the previous year. Last year levels among the one-offs fell back to average for most drugs apart from cannabis and LSD, and frequent/regular use of Class A drugs was no different to the 'nevers'.

Table 4.3:   Percentage of runaways using drugs in their lifetime and the last year (aged 12 to 30)

	Lifetime			Last year		
	Serial	One-off	Never a	Serial	One-off	Never a
	runaway	runaway	runaway	runaway	runaway	runaway
Amphetamine	***56	***31	19	***32	10	8
Cannabis	***78	***65	38	***54	***47	23
Cocaine	***23	10	8	**11	5	4
Crack	***8	3	1	1	1	-
Ecstasy	***31	*15	9	8	5	4
Heroin	***7	3	1	**4	1	-
LSD	***38	***23	11	***8	**5	2
Mushrooms	***27	***19	9	***9	5	2
Methadone	***5	*3	1	1	1	-
Poppers	***35	*23	15	***16	3	3
Solvents	***41	***19	7	***8	1	1
Steroids	1	0	1	0	0	-
Tranquillisers	***19	6	3	***8	2	1
Any drug	***82	***68	42	***55	***46	25
Monthly Class A	NA	NA	NA	**8	3	2
Unweighted (n)	125	161	4,490	119	160	4,399

Source: YLS weighted data. * p<0.05; ** p<0.01; *** p<0.001 using Pearson's χ^2 or Fisher's Exact Test, where appropriate, performed on 'serial runaways' and 'one-off runaways' versus 'never runaway'. '-' = less than 0.5%. 'Monthly Class A' is defined as 'use of any Class A drug at least once a month in the last year'. NA = not applicable (as monthly use is over the last year). All data presented in this report for runaways refer to 12- to 30-year-olds (at time of interview).

Table 4.4 examines differences in more recent drug use among the runaway groups by sex. Serial runaways appeared to have very high levels of use in the last year for all types of drug. In absolute terms, male serial runaways had the highest levels, with one in eleven using heroin and one in six cocaine, but female serial runaways had higher levels of use compared to their counterparts who had never run away – though not for the most harmful drugs. Only female serial runaways were regularly using Class A drugs on a significantly greater basis than their counterparts who had not run away from home. This reflects the findings among young offenders in Chapter 3. The only significant differences between the one-off runaways and those never doing so, were the higher rates of cannabis and 'any drug' use for both male and female (one-off) runaways, together with greater use of LSD among males.

Table 4.4: **_Percentage of runaways using drugs in the last year by sex (aged 12 to 30)_**

	Serial runaway		One-off runaway		Never a runaway	
	Male	Female	Male	Female	Male	Female
Amphetamine	***38	***28	16	6	10	6
Cannabis	***64	***47	***52	***43	28	19
Cocaine	**17	7	10	3	6	2
Crack	2	0	2	0	1	-
Ecstasy	*17	2	8	2	6	2
Heroin	***9	0	2	0	1	-
LSD	**11	***7	**10	2	2	1
Mushrooms	*11	**7	7	2	4	1
Methadone	2	0	2	0	-	-
Poppers	**17	***16	5	1	4	2
Solvents	*9	***8	2	1	2	1
Steroids	0	0	0	0	1	0
Tranquillisers	***13	**7	2	2	1	1
Any drug	***63	***47	**48	***44	31	20
Monthly Class A	8	***8	5	2	3	1
Unweighted n	43	76	58	102	2,088	2,311

Source: YLS weighted data. * $p<0.05$; ** $p<0.01$; *** $p<0.001$ using Pearson's χ^2 or Fisher's Exact Test, where appropriate, performed on 'serial runaways' and 'one-off runaways' versus 'never runaway' for 'males' and 'females'. '-' = less than 0.5%. 'Monthly Class A' is defined as 'use of any Class A drug at least once a month in the last year.' NA = not applicable (as monthly use is over the last year).

Discussion

Drug dependence was reported by 41 per cent of homeless young people aged 16 to 24 in a study carried out in Glasgow (Kershaw *et al.*, 2000). In the USA, rates of drug use and abuse were found to be two to three times higher among runaway and homeless youth than for young people in school, and their attitudes to drug use were considerably more tolerant (Fors and Rojek, 1991; Greene *et al.*, 1997). These groups are therefore particularly in need of targeted prevention and treatment programmes (Forst, 1994), especially as runaway and homeless youths also using drugs appear to be at greater risk of attempting suicide, even after controlling for key demographic characteristics (Greene and Ringwalt, 1996). The Prime Minister has recently asked the Social Exclusion Unit to look into the problems of young runaways as a potential area for future work with a view to developing a National Service Framework for this vulnerable group (SEU, 2001).

The YLS can provide only partial information on runaways and particularly the homeless, as it is a survey of those living in households. Nevertheless, it corroborates the higher rates of lifetime, last year and monthly Class A drug use on the part of those ever sleeping rough or running away from home several times when under sixteen. There were differing degrees of vulnerability within the two groups, which seemed to interact with gender. Rough sleepers and serial runaways had much higher rates of drug use, especially of more harmful drugs, than those reporting homelessness without sleeping rough or just a single episode of running away from home. Homeless and runaway females had relatively higher prevalence rates compared with their non-vulnerable counterparts, although males had the highest absolute rates. Higher prevalence seemed to persist into later life, even when episodes of homelessness and running away may have occurred some time in the past. It must be remembered, though, that the young homeless are not a homogeneous mass. Consequently, risk factors, mental health and substance use will all vary within this group (Adlaf and Zdanowicz, 1999). The complex links between homelessness, drug use and mental health (particularly depression) are only beginning to be understood. Treatment for the latter two conditions may be required in combination and carried out as an 'assertive outreach service' to be most effective (Wrate and Blair, 1999). Evaluations of such programmes appear promising but there is some evidence that reductions in drug abuse may be short-lived (Craig and Timms, 2000).

5   Living in drug-using families

Introduction

It has been argued that family and peer influences on young peoples' drug use are paramount (ACMD, 1998), although the exact causal mechanisms and interactions with other factors, such as genetics and social exclusion, are uncertain. There has been a relatively recent concentration in the research literature on the family as the main influence on the initiation and escalation of adolescent drug use and, in particular, on the effects of home environment, family relationships and parenting styles (Swadi, 1999). However, much of this (largely North American) research on juvenile delinquency has been criticised for being 'disjointed and contradictory' and lacking a sound theoretical and methodological basis (ACMD, 1998: p.34). Its application to the UK context should therefore be treated carefully.

Linking the YLS and the BCS

It is possible to link the responses in the YLS to those in the BCS through a unique household identification number. There was a substantial overlap of households sampled in the YLS and the 1998 BCS. Additionally, a variable in the YLS dataset recorded the relationship of the respondent to the BCS respondent, where this was applicable. Almost 2,300 relatives living with the original BCS respondents were interviewed in the YLS, with around three-quarters being sons or daughters.

Hence, we can examine the effects of drug use among parents (reporting to the BCS) on the drug use of their children (reporting to the YLS). Sibling effects, which seemed to be stronger still, can also be assessed – although the smaller numbers here allowed less detailed analysis. Drug use among partners who live together remains outside this report's focus on vulnerable groups. The relationships between respondents in the same households are summarised in Table 5.1 below. A fair number of the interviews (31% of households in both surveys) were conducted with the same person.

Bearing these points in mind, it is plain from analysis of the YLS and BCS, that drug use is concentrated within households on several levels, for there were strong associations in prevalence between parents and their children, spouses, co-habitees and siblings. Overall, nearly half of YLS respondents living with a relative who had used drugs had used a drug themselves, compared to only a third without such a family member (see Table 5.1). Interestingly, unrelated respondents living in the same household did not have significantly different levels of use – around half had used a drug whether their fellow householders had or not.

Table 5.1: Relationships of YLS respondent to BCS respondent and associated lifetime drug use

Relation of YLS to BCS respondent	Unweighted (n)	%	% ever using any drug if fellow householder had:	
			Ever used a drug	Never used a drug
Partners				
Husband/wife	229	6	**54	35
Co-habitee	165	6	*67	50
Children				
Son/daughter¶	1,670	46	*41	33
Son/daughter-in-law‡	14	-	-	-
Siblings				
Brother/sister¶	174	7	***43	20
Brother/sister-in-law‡	3	-	-	-
Other relation	26	1	-	-
Total related	2,281	65	***48	33
Same respondent	1,232	31	NA	NA
Unrelated	79	3	52	55
Missing data‡	9	-	-	-
Total	3,601	100	NA	NA

Source: YLS weighted (percentages) and unweighted (frequencies) data. ¶Includes adopted/step/foster. ‡Small sample sizes preclude analysis. * $p<0.05$; ** $p<0.01$; *** $p<0.001$ using Pearson's χ^2 or Fisher's Exact Test, where appropriate. '-' = less than 0.5%. NA = not applicable.

Living with a drug-using parent

Introduction

Research, largely undertaken in the USA, has demonstrated that parental attitudes to and use of drugs are significant factors in the initiation of adolescent drug use (Hoffmann and Su, 1998a), although these may not be as strong as older sibling or peer group effects (Aseltine, 1995; Swadi, 1988). Peers and, to a lesser extent, older siblings have been found to be sources of drug supply for youngsters, as well as co-drug users (Needle *et al.*, 1986). A research review concluded that factors relating to the family were particularly important in progression to problematic drug use (Ovendon *et al.*, 1993) and this was corroborated by Hoffmann *et al.* (2000), where higher levels of parent-child attachment served to diminish adolescent drug-using careers. Additionally, cross-generational drug use within families may have a 'normalising' effect on young peoples' attitudes and use (Brown, 1989). There is even some evidence of drug type-specific, sociological risk factors for family influences on drug use (Merikangas *et al.*, 1998).

Brook *et al.* (1999) found that drug use of younger brothers was linked, independently of other factors, to the drug use of and their relationships with parents and older brothers. Indeed, such family dynamics may have a complex interactive effect in association with peer influences (Swadi, 1988), and gender-specific, 'stressful life events' (Hoffmann and Su, 1998b). The constitution of and gender roles within families can play a part. For instance, peer clusters may be the more important factor for drug-using girls and for adolescents of both sexes in homes without a father or stepfather (Farrell and White, 1998). Also, Reinherz *et al.* (2000) found effects of parental substance abuse on sons' but not daughters' drug use and French researchers found that living with both parents and having a non-working mother were protective factors in their sample of 2,400 school children (Challier *et al.*, 2000). Class may also interact with family and peer influences, where, for instance, in a re-analysis of the US 'Monitoring the Future' school survey, the protective nature of religiosity was enhanced for 'upper class' adolescents and peer influences were stronger for middle classes (McGee, 1992). Religion's role as a protective factor, particularly in the UK rather than the US, is not without controversy (see Ramsay and Percy, 1996: p.66). Nonetheless, recent analysis of the 1994 and 1996 BCS has shown religious practice to be an important protective factor for all types of drug use (MacDonald, 2000).

However, differences in family structure (e.g. number of parents lived with) were noted to be relatively unimportant by Brody and Forehand (1993) in forecasting substance abuse, compared to family process (e.g. having parents who constantly argue). The Advisory Council on the Misuse of Drugs confirms this view, and that "... warmth, affection, consistency, and parental supervision are the most reliable indicators of effective parenting" (1998: p.35), rather than the 'broken home' concept, which appears to have been used inconsistently in previous deviance literature.

Parents and children

Only 53 parents (3%) who were BCS respondents, with children who took part in the YLS, had used a drug in the last year; 338 (21%) had ever done so. Those parents who had ever used a drug were slightly younger (mean age 42) than those who had not (mean age 44). Prevalence figures were broadly similar to those in the 1998 BCS for 40- to 44-year-olds, where 25 per cent had used ever used an illicit drug. Just less than one per cent of the sample of parents were under 30, and the ratio of males to females was approximately two to three. This could lead to an understating of drug use overall within this group (as drug prevalence rates for males are generally found to be higher).

Nearly two-thirds of the BCS respondent's children were under 18, and only six per cent were over 25. Overall, the gender split was broadly even among the children, but there were more males in the older groups (e.g. 65% of the over-21s). The split between fathers, mothers, sons and daughters was again relatively equitable, the largest group being the mother-son pairing (31%) and the father-daughter pair the smallest (18%).

In all four types of parent-child dyad, parental use of any drug in the last year was associated with a higher prevalence of lifetime use of any drug among children, but with a significant difference ($p<0.05$ using Pearson's χ^2 Test) only for the mother-son pairing (see Table 5.2).

Table 5.2: Percentage of children using drugs in their lifetime by the comparative gender of parents and their children

Parent-child pairing	Parent used any drug ever	Parent never used a drug	Parent used any drug last year	Parent not used any drug last year	Unweighted n
Mother-son	49	39	**40	25	468
Mother-daughter	38	29	28	21	447
Father-son	37	34	28	19	352
Father-daughter	37	29	24	19	283

Source: YLS and BCS weighted data. * $p<0.05$; ** $p<0.01$; *** $p<0.001$ using Pearson's χ^2 Test.

Use of the more harmful drugs among parents was rare and cannabis was the drug most commonly used last year (2%) and ever (15%). Amphetamine (4%), tranquillisers (3%) and 'smoked something unknown' (3%) – usually assumed to be cannabis (Ramsay and Partridge, 1999; Mott and Mirrlees-Black, 1995), although some other drugs are also smokeable, e.g. cocaine – were the only other categories featuring at rates higher than one in 50 on a lifetime basis. No drugs other than cannabis were used by more than half a per cent of parents during the previous year.

Table 5.3 outlines the percentage of children using different types of drug ever and in the last year for those with and without parents who had ever used a drug. Lifetime parental drug use had a significant association with children's lifetime use of crack, cannabis and tranquillisers. There was no statistically significant difference in the proportions using Class A drugs on a monthly basis. Of those with a parental lifetime user, nearly one in six were using a drug monthly over the previous year, compared to one in ten without. Significantly higher proportions of children with parental drug users had taken cannabis and amphetamine during the last year.

Table 5.3: *Percentage of children, with a parent who had ever/never used drugs, using drugs in their lifetime and the last year*

| | % children using lifetime | | % children using last year | |
	Parent used any ever	Parent never used	Parent used any ever	Parent never used
Amphetamine	17	13	*10	6
Cannabis	**37	29	***30	20
Cocaine	6	4	3	2
Crack	*3	1	-	-
Ecstasy	7	5	4	3
Heroin	2	1	0	1
LSD	8	7	1	2
Mushrooms	8	6	2	2
Methadone	1	1	0	-
Poppers	11	12	2	4
Solvents	8	7	2	2
Steroids	1	1	-	-
Tranquillisers	*5	3	3	1
Any drug	*41	33	***31	22
Monthly Class A	NA	NA	4	2
Unweighted n	*338*	*1,212*	*338*	*1,212*

Source: YLS and BCS weighted data. * $p<0.05$; ** $p<0.01$; *** $p<0.001$ using Pearson's χ^2, or Fisher's Exact Test where appropriate, on children with a parental lifetime drug user compared to those without. '-' = less than 0.5%. 'Monthly Class A' is defined as 'use of any Class A drug at least once a month in the last year'. NA = not applicable (as monthly use is over the last year).

The effect of a parent using drugs more recently (i.e. in the last year) was even less striking, and only children's lifetime ecstasy use was significantly higher (see Table 5.4); however, numbers were small for parents using drugs in the last year. This makes it hard to draw clear conclusions. Generally though, rates of lifetime drug use among children of last year parental users were often double that of the 'non-vulnerable' group. Parental use of drugs in the last year appeared to have no readily discernible effect on their children's use over the same period.

Table 5.4: *Percentage of children, with a parent who had/had not used drugs in the last year, using drugs in their lifetime and the last year*

	% children using lifetime		% children using last year	
	Parent used any last year	Parent did not use any last year	Parent used any last year	Parent did not use any last year
Amphetamine	16	14	9	7
Cannabis	31	30	27	22
Cocaine	7	4	4	3
Crack	0	1	0	-
Ecstasy	*13	5	7	3
Heroin	2	1	0	1
LSD	13	7	2	1
Mushrooms	13	6	2	2
Methadone	2	1	0	-
Poppers	16	11	0	3
Solvents	13	7	4	2
Steroids	0	1	0	-
Tranquillisers	7	3	0	2
Monthly Class A	NA	NA	2	2
Any drug	34	35	28	24
Unweighted n	*53*	*1,497*	*53*	*1,497*

Source: YLS and BCS weighted (percentages) and unweighted (base) data. * $p<0.05$; ** $p<0.01$; *** $p<0.001$ using Pearson's χ^2, or Fisher's Exact Test where appropriate, on children with a parental last year drug user compared to those without. '-' = less than 0.5%. 'Monthly Class A' is defined as 'use of any Class A drug at least once a month in the last year'. NA = not applicable (as monthly use is over the last year).

Access

In parallel with the findings on recent parental drug use, there appeared to be no substantial differences in perceptions of access to different drugs between children whose parents had ever and never used drugs.

The proportion of respondents who could not answer about the accessibility of the selected drugs was slightly lower universally for the offspring of parents using drugs more recently (in the last year) compared to children without a parental lifetime user. This may indicate that children have greater knowledge about drugs and drug markets in general if their parents are recent users of drugs (albeit mostly cannabis). This effect was not apparent if the parent had used drugs ever, rather than in the last year, as one might expect. However, bivariate reclassification of the access questions into "don't knows" versus all the other answers indicating at least some knowledge of drug markets (i.e. very easy, fairly easy, fairly difficult, very difficult and "it varies") did not give rise to any statistically significant associations. In other words, the data did not support the hypothesis relating to an association between parental drug use and children's enhanced knowledge of drug markets.

Finally, nearly one in five children living with recent, drug-using parents thought that ecstasy was very easy to get hold of, compared to nearly one in eight without. Again, this was not statistically significant, but may tie in with the higher lifetime prevalence of ecstasy use among children of drug-using parents (13% versus 5%) shown in Table 5.5.

Drug use among siblings

As was shown in Table 5.1, the relationship between siblings' drug use seemed to be the most pronounced – more so than between parents and children. If a brother or sister in the BCS reported ever using any drug, 43 per cent of their (older or younger) siblings in the YLS also reported taking them, compared to only 20 per cent if they had not. One would expect differences to be dependent on the relative age and gender of siblings, as found in, for instance, Brook et al.'s (1999) work on brothers, although detailed analyses of sub-groups and even drug types are heavily restricted by the small sample size.

It was not possible to work out the exact relative ages of siblings, as dates of birth were not recorded in either survey and the information on 1998 BCS interview dates is unreliable for individual cases. However, we have assumed that if the age reported by the interviewee in the BCS was the same or greater than that reported by the linked interviewee in the YLS, then the BCS respondent was the older sibling, otherwise the YLS respondent was older. This also assumes there were no twins! The responses were then combined, giving a total sample of 172 sibling pairs with a reasonably even combination of relative age and genders, although two cases had missing values for age. The siblings were arranged into "older" and "younger" groups purely as a matter of convenience – we are not implying that older siblings will always lead and influence their younger brothers and sisters, even if this may often be the case in practice (Needle, 1986).

The percentages of younger siblings who used drugs with and without an older sibling drug user are shown in Table 5.5. Approximately equal proportions of older siblings (37%; n=67) and younger siblings (36%; n=58) had ever used a drug. The majority of younger siblings who had ever used a drug (76%) were over sixteen, so age should not have confounded the relationships unduly. Indeed, after breaking down responses by age group, the relationship still held. For instance, a third of younger siblings aged 12 to 16 had ever used a drug if their older brother or sister had also done so (see Table 5.5). Only one in ten of the same age group had ever taken a drug if their elder sibling had not. The effect of having an elder drug-using sibling was proportionately more pronounced for 12-to 16-year-olds, but older groups had the higher absolute rates. Rates of use of any drug in the last year were up to eight times higher for 12- to 16-year-olds with a sibling drug-user compared to those without, but less than twice as high for the 17-plus group. A second effect was that having an older sibling using drugs more recently (in the last year) meant that higher rates were also observed among the younger siblings for their use in the previous year (see Table 5.6).

Table 5.5: *Percentage of younger siblings using drugs in their lifetime and the last year with/without an older sibling lifetime drug user*

	Younger sibling used any drug ever		Younger sibling used any drug in the last year	
	Older sibling used ever	Older sibling never used	Older sibling used ever	Older sibling never used
Younger sibling aged 12-16	**33	10	**23	3
Younger sibling aged 17+	**68	40	35	22
Unweighted bases	*33*	*47*	*33*	*46*
	34	*58*	*34*	*57*

Source: YLS and BCS weighted data. * p<0.05; ** p<0.01; *** p<0.001 using Pearson's χ^2 test or Fisher's Exact Test, where appropriate, comparing younger siblings with and without older sibling drug users.

Table 5.6: *Percentage of younger siblings using drugs in their lifetime and the last year with/without an older sibling last year drug user*

	Younger sibling used any drug ever		Younger sibling used any drug in the last year	
	Older sibling used last year	Older sibling did not use last year	Older sibling used last year	Older sibling did not use last year
Younger sibling aged 12-16	**42	14	**32	6
Younger sibling aged 17+	***79	42	**46	21
Unweighted bases	*17*	*63*	*17*	*62*
	21	*70*	*21*	*69*

Source: YLS and BCS weighted data. * p<0.05; ** p<0.01; *** p<0.001 using Pearson's χ^2 test or Fisher's Exact Test, where appropriate, comparing younger siblings with and without older sibling drug users.

Discussion

The analyses presented in this chapter clearly show associations of drug use between members of families living in the same household, and particularly between different siblings and between parents and children. This was not the case for unrelated household members. However, compared with other vulnerable groups discussed in this report, the associations across the generations in particular were not especially strong. This may have been because recent drug use among parents in this sample was quite rare and generally restricted to cannabis. This in turn may reflect the fact that, as commonly acknowledged in the literature, parenthood is regarded as a protective factor for personal drug use. As noted by Ramsay and Percy (1996), for instance, "many traditional roles and responsibilities, such as entering the labour market and setting up home with a partner, appear to be associated with abstention from drug use". It may also be the case that children are more willing to admit to their own drug use if they are aware that their parents are occasional cannabis smokers, for instance.

In so far as parental drug use did have some effect on the drug use of their children, this was more apparent in terms of lifetime parental use of any drug, which seemed to be associated with increased use of some drugs. The sibling data pointed to further contrasts, where recent use by older siblings was associated with higher rates among their younger brothers and sisters. The rates of drug use among those with an older sibling who had never used drugs were very low indeed, at three per cent for lifetime use of any drug, for instance. This concurs with Goddard and Higgins' (2000) findings, where 39 per cent of school children aged 11 to 15 had ever used drugs if they knew a sibling also used drugs, compared to five per cent if not. When broken down by the relative genders of parents and children, only the mother-son pairing showed statistically significant associations in drug use (see Table 5.2). More qualitative work is needed to clarify the reasons behind such connections and the interactions of gender, age and family relationships. The Prevention Working Group of the Advisory Council on the Misuse of Drugs is considering the issue of parental (albeit primarily problematic) drug use, which should provide important information in this complex area and importantly, issue firm recommendations for policy and practice within the UK context.

6   **Conclusion**

The preceding chapters have shown generally higher levels of use of a range of drug types by groups of young people who:

- have truanted or been excluded from school
- have committed crimes
- have been homeless
- have runaway from home
- live with a familial drug-user

Rates of use were generally higher for these groups in comparison to their "non-vulnerable" counterparts, although it was not always possible to control for other potentially confounding factors. Where this was done, in terms of age and sex, the relationships usually remained. Access to drugs was also generally perceived to be easier by members of the vulnerable groups examined in this report.

An important finding from this analysis has concerned the interaction between gender and 'vulnerability', particularly among the younger groups of truants and excludees. Here, rates of drug use among excludees – the more disaffected of the two groups – who were girls were invariably higher than those for boys. These findings were based on relatively small samples, however, and can only point to the need for further research to help elucidate the underlying processes. Other research has also indicated high levels of drug use (including opiates and cocaine) among females at the margins of mainstream society – for example, female offenders (Bennett, 2000) and school excludees (Powis et al., 1998). Therefore, it is especially important to discover how far girls under sixteen are at risk of progressing to problematic use of the more harmful drugs. We must reiterate that we have concentrated in this report on the broadest categories of drug use and not on the development of more extreme forms of drug misuse and dependence among vulnerable young people.

Vulnerability to drug use may also change over time and within the categories used in this report. We have tried to show that there are degrees of offending, school exclusion, homelessness and so on that are associated with corresponding increases in the use of illicit drugs among young people – that is, there is no easy dichotomy between 'the vulnerable' and the 'non-vulnerable'. We have also seen that some of those who have experienced the most extreme types of social exclusion, such as sleeping rough, have been able to resolve some of their social difficulties (i.e. a return to some kind of home), even if many continue to use drugs at least 'recreationally'.

This report has helped to extend knowledge of patterns of drug use among vulnerable youth. It is intended to inform the Government's anti-drugs strategy and the forthcoming programme of quantitative and qualitative research, concentrating on particular vulnerable groups, which will report during 2002/03. The tracking of the performance of the Government's anti-drugs strategy should continue to include a focus on groups of young people at particularly high risk of developing problematic drug use. Our analysis shows that serious and persistent offenders, rough sleepers, serial runaways and those disaffected with school have particularly high prevalence rates for all drug types and that there may be an important interaction between vulnerability and gender for younger age groups.

Adamczuk, H. (2000) 'Drug misuse, cigarette smoking and alcohol use', in Evans, K. and Alade, S. (Eds.) *Vulnerable young people and drugs: opportunities to tackle inequalities.* London: DrugScope.

Adlaf, E.M. and Zdanowicz, Y.M. (1999) 'A cluster-analytic study of substance problems and mental health among street youths', *American Journal of Drug and Alcohol Abuse*, 25(4): 639-60.

Advisory Council on the Misuse of Drugs (ACMD) (1982) Treatment and Rehabilitation. London: The Stationery Office.

Advisory Council on the Misuse of Drugs (ACMD) (1998) Drug Misuse and the Environment. London: The Stationery Office.

Aldridge, J., Parker, H. and Measham, F. (1999) *Drug trying and drug use across adolescence – a longitudinal study of young people's drug taking in two regions of northern England.* DPAS Paper 1. London: Home Office.

Aseltine, R.H. Jr. (1995) 'A reconsideration of parental and peer influences on adolescent deviance', *Journal of Health and Social Behavior*, 36(2): 103-21.

Audit Commission (1996) *Misspent youth: young people and crime.* London: Audit Commission.

Aye Maung, N. (1995) 'Survey design and interpretation of the British Crime Survey', in Walker, M. (Ed.) *Interpreting crime statistics.* Oxford: Oxford University Press.

Balding, J. (2000) *Young people and illegal drugs into 2000.* Exeter: Schools Health Education Unit.

Bennett, T. (1998) *Drugs and crime: the results of research on drug testing and interviewing arrestees.* Home Office Research Study 183. London: Home Office.

Bennett, T. (2000) *Drugs and crime: the results of the second developmental stage of the NEW-ADAM programme.* Home Office Research Study 205. London: Home Office.

Boys, A., Fountain, J., Marsden, J., Griffiths, P., Stillwell, G. and Strang, J. (2000) *Drugs decisions: a qualitative study of young people.* London: Health Education Authority.

Brody, G.H. and Forehand, R. (1993) 'Prospective associations among family form, family processes, and adolescents' alcohol and drug use', *Behavioral Research Therapy,* 31(6): 587-93.

Brook, J.S., Brook, D.W. and Whiteman, M. (1999) 'Older sibling correlates of younger sibling drug use in the context of parent-child relations', *Genetic, Social and General Psychology Monographs,* 125(4): 451-68.

Brown, S.A. (1989) 'Life events of adolescents in relation to personal and parental substance abuse', *American Journal of Psychiatry,* 146(4): 484-9.

Bryman, A. and Cramer, D. (1994) *Quantitative data analysis for social scientists (revised edition).* London and New York: Routledge.

Carlen, P. (1996) *Jigsaw: a political criminology of youth homelessness.* Buckingham and Philadelphia: Open University Press.

Challier, B., Chau, N., Predine, R., Choquet, M. and Legras, B. (2000) 'Associations of family environment and individual factors with tobacco, alcohol, and illicit drug use in adolescents', *European Journal of Epidemiology,* 16(1): 33-42.

Children's Society (1999) *Runaway child: an advice leaflet for parents and carers.* http://www.the-childrens-society.org.uk/download/index_download.html

Craig, T.K. and Hodson, S. (1998) 'Homeless youth in London: I. Childhood antecedents and psychiatric disorder', *Psychological Medicine,* 28(6): 1379-88.

Craig, T.K. and Hodson, S. (2000) 'Homeless youth in London: II. Accommodation, employment and health outcomes at 1 year', *Psychological Medicine,* 30(1): 187-94.

Craig, T.K. and Timms, P. (2000) 'Facing up to social exclusion: services for homeless mentally ill people', *International Review of Psychiatry,* 12: 206-11.

Desai, R.A., Lam, J. and Rosenheck, R.A. (2000) 'Childhood risk factors for criminal justice involvement in a sample of homeless people with serious mental illness', *Journal of Nervous and Mental Disease,* 188(6): 324-32.

Edmunds, M., Hough, M., Turnbull, P.J. and May, T. (1999) *Doing justice to treatment: referring offenders to drug services.* DPAS Paper 2. London: Home Office.

Edmunds, M., May, T.M., Hearnden, I. and Hough, M. (1998) *Arrest Referral: emerging lessons from research.* DPI Paper 23. London: Home Office.

Egginton, R. and Parker, H. (2000) *Hidden heroin users: young people's unchallenged journeys to problematic drug use.* London: DrugScope.

Evans, A. (1996) *We don't choose to be homeless: report of the national inquiry into preventing youth homelessness.* London: CHAR.

Evans, K. and Alade, S. (2000) *Vulnerable young people and drugs: opportunities to tackle inequalities.* London: DrugScope.

Farrell, A.D. and White, K.S. (1998) 'Peer influences and drug use among urban adolescents: family structure and parent-adolescent relationship as protective factors', *Journal of Consultant and Clinical Psychology,* 66(2): 248-58.

Fisher, N., Turner, S.W., Pugh, R. and Taylor, C. (1994) 'Estimated numbers of homeless and non-homeless mentally ill people in north east Westminster by using capture-recapture analysis', *British Medical Journal,* 308: 27-30.

Flemen, K. (1997) *Smoke and whispers: drugs and youth homelessness in central London.* London: The Hungerford Drugs Project.

Flood-Page, C., Campbell, S., Harrington, V. and Miller, J. (2000) *Youth crime: findings from the 1998/1999 Youth Lifestyles Survey.* Home Office Research Study 209. London: Home Office.

Fors, S.W. and Rojek, D.G. (1991) 'A comparison of drug involvement between runaways and school youths', *Journal of Drug Education,* 21(1): 13-25.

Forst, M.L. (1994) 'A substance use profile of delinquent and homeless youths', *Journal of Drug Education,* 24(3): 219-31.

Goddard, E. and Higgins, V. (1999) *Smoking, drinking and drug use among young teenagers in 1998.* London: Office for National Statistics.

Goddard, E. and Higgins, V. (2000) *Drug use, smoking and drinking among young teenagers in 1999.* London: Office for National Statistics.

Gossop, M., Marsden, J. and Stewart, D. (1998) *NTORS at one year: changes in substance use, health and criminal behaviour one year after intake.* London: Department of Health.

Goulden, C., Ramsay, M., Sibbitt, R. and Sondhi, A. (forthcoming chapter in Home Office review) *Gearing drugs policy to crime reduction: evidence from research.*

Graham, J. and Bowling, B. (1995) *Young people and crime.* Home Office Research Study 145. London: Home Office.

Greene, J.M. and Ringwalt, C.L. (1996) 'Youth and familial substance use's association with suicide attempts among runaway and homeless youth', *Substance Use and Misuse,* 31(8): 1041-58.

Greene, J.M., Ennett, S.T. and Ringwalt, C.L. (1997) 'Substance use among runaway and homeless youth in three national samples', *American Journal of Public Health,* 87(2): 229-35.

Hall, W. (2000) 'The cannabis policy debate: finding a way forward', *Canadian Medical Association Journal,* 162: 1690-2.

Health Advisory Service (HAS) (1996) *Children and young people: substance misuse services the substance of young need.* London: Stationery Office.

Heffron, W.A., Skipper, B.J. and Lambert, L. (1997) 'Health and lifestyle issues as risk factors for homelessness', *Journal of the American Board of Family Practitioners,* 10(1): 6-12.

Hoffmann, J.P. and Su, S.S. (1998a) 'Parental substance use disorder, mediating variables and adolescent drug use: a non-recursive model', *Addiction,* 93(9): 1351-64.

Hoffmann, J.P. and Su, S.S. (1998b) 'Stressful life events and adolescent substance use and depression: conditional and gender differentiated effects', *Substance Use and Misuse,* 33(11): 2219-62.

Hoffmann, J.P., Cerbone, F.G. and Su, S.S. (2000) 'A growth curve analysis of stress and adolescent drug use', *Substance Use and Misuse,* 35(5): 687-716.

Hough, M. (1996) *Problem drug use and criminal justice: a review of the literature.* Central Drugs Prevention Unit: Paper No. 15. London: Home Office.

Hoyt, G.M. and Chaloupka, F.J. (1994) 'Effect of survey conditions on self-reported substance use', *Contemporary Economic Policy,* 12, 109-121.

Kershaw, A., Singleton, N. and Meltzer, H. (2000) *Substance misuse and mental disorder among homeless people in Glasgow.* http://www.statistics.gov.uk/nsbase/pdfdir/sub0300.pdf

Kipke, M.D., Montgomery, S.B., Simon, T.R. and Iverson, E.F. (1997) '"Substance abuse" disorders among runaway and homeless youth', *Substance Use and Misuse,* 32(7-8): 969-86.

Lawrenson, F. (1997) 'Runaway children: whose problem?', *British Medical Journal,* 314 (7087): 1064.

Lloyd, C. (1998) 'Risk factors for problem drug use: identifying vulnerable groups', *Drugs: education, prevention and policy,* 5(3): 217-232.

Lloyd, C. and Griffiths, P. (1998) 'Editorial: Problems for the future? Drug use among vulnerable groups of young people', *Drugs: education, prevention and policy,* 5(3): 213-216.

MacDonald, Z. (2000) 'The determinants of illicit drug use', in MacDonald, Z. and Pyle, D. (Eds.) *Illicit activity: the economics of crime, drugs and tax fraud.* Dartmouth: Ashgate.

MacLeod, M. (1997) 'Responsibility for services for runaway children must be shared', *British Medical Journal,* 315 (7103): 312.

McGee, Z.T. (1992) 'Social class differences in parental and peer influence on adolescent drug use', *Deviant Behavior,* 13: 349-372.

Merikangas, K.R., Stolar, M., Stevens, G.E., Goulet, J., Preisig, M.A., Fenton, B., Zhang, H., O'Malley, S.S. and Rounsaville, B.J. (1998) 'Familial transmission of substance use disorders', *Archives of General Psychiatry,* 55(11): 973-9.

Miller, P. and Plant, M. (1999) 'Truancy and perceived school performance: an alcohol and drug study of UK teenagers', *Alcohol and Alcoholism,* 34(6): 886-93.

Misuse of Drugs Act (1971). London: Stationery Office.

Mott, J. and Mirrlees-Black, C. (1995) *Self-reported drug misuse in England and Wales: findings from the 1992 British Crime Survey.* Research and Planning Unit Paper 89. London: Home Office.

Needle, R., McCubbin, H., Wilson, M., Reineck, R., Lazar, A. and Mederer, H. (1986) 'Interpersonal influences in adolescent drug use – the role of older siblings, parents and peers', *International Journal of Addiction,* 21(7): 739-66.

Newburn, T. (1998) 'Young offenders, drugs and prevention', *Drugs: education, prevention and policy,* 5(3): 233-244.

Norusis, M.J. (1994) SPSS® Professional Statistics (Version 6.1). Chicago: SPSS Inc.

Norusis, M.J. (1998) SPSS® Base 8.0 Applications Guide. Chicago: SPSS Inc.

Ovendon, C., Marsh, A. and Loxley, W. (1993) *Problematic drug use: factors associated with heavy drug use and injecting drug use in adolescents.* Curtin University of Technology: National Centre for Research into the Prevention of Drug Abuse.

Plant, M. and Miller, P. (2000) 'Drug use has declined among teenagers in United Kingdom', *British Medical Journal,* 320: 1536.

Powis, B., Griffiths, P., Gossop M., Lloyd, C. and Strang, J. (1998) 'Drug use and offending behaviour among young people excluded from school', *Drugs: education, prevention and policy,* 5(3): 245-56.

Ramsay, M. and Partridge, S. (1999) *Drug misuse declared in 1998: results from the British Crime Survey.* Home Office Research Study 197. London: Home Office.

Ramsay, M. and Percy, A. (1996) *Drug misuse declared: results of the 1994 British Crime Survey.* Home Office Research Study 151. London: Home Office.

Reinherz, H.Z., Giaconia, R.M., Hauf, A.M., Wasserman, M.S. and Paradis, A.D. (2000) 'General and specific childhood risk factors for depression and drug disorders by early adulthood', *Journal of the American Academy of Child and Adolescent Psychiatry,* 39(2): 223-31.

Royal College of Psychiatrists (RCP) (2000) *Drugs, dilemmas and choices: a working party of the Royal College of Psychiatrists and the Royal College of Physicians.* London: Gaskell.

Rugg, J. (2000) *Making connections: tackling youth homelessness through a multi-agency strategy.* London: Shelter.

Schaffner, L. (1998) 'Searching for connection: a new look at teenaged runaways', *Adolescence,* 33(131): 619-27.

Shanks, N.J., George, S.L., Westlake, L. and al-Kalai, D. (1994) 'Who are the homeless?', *Public Health,* 108(1): 11-19.

Social Exclusion Unit (SEU) (1998a) *Truancy and school exclusion.* London: Stationery Office.

Social Exclusion Unit (SEU) (1998b) *Rough sleeping.* London: Stationery Office.

Social Exclusion Unit (SEU) (2001) *Consultation on young runaways: background paper by the Social Exclusion Unit.* London: Cabinet Office.

Stiffman, A.R. (1989) 'Physical and sexual abuse in runaway youths', *Child Abuse and Neglect,* 13(3): 417-26.

Stratford, N. and Roth, W. (1999) *The 1998 Youth Lifestyles Survey: technical report.* London: National Centre for Social Research.

Swadi, H. (1999) 'Individual risk factors for adolescent substance use', *Drug and Alcohol Dependency,* 55(3): 209-24.

Swadi, H.S. (1988) 'Adolescent drug-taking: the role of family and peers', *Drug and Alcohol Dependency,* 21(2): 157-60.

United Kingdom Anti-Drugs Co-ordination Unit (UKADCU) (1998) *Tackling drugs to build a better Britain: the Government's 10-year strategy for tackling drug misuse.* London: Cabinet Office.

United Kingdom Anti-Drugs Co-ordination Unit (UKADCU) (2000) *Tackling drugs to build a better Britain: second national plan 2000/2001.* London: Cabinet Office.

Wade, G. and Barnett, T. (1999) 'Homelessness, drugs and young people', in Marlow, A. and Pearson, G. (Eds.) *Young people, drugs and community safety.* Dorset: Russell House Publishing.

White, C. and Lewis, J. (1998) *Following up the British Crime Survey 1996: a qualitative study.* London: SCPR.

Wrate, R. and Blair, C. (1999) 'Homeless adolescents', in Vostanis, P. and Cumella, S. (Eds.) *Homeless children: problems and needs.* London and Philadelphia: Jessica Kingsley.

Wright, J.D. and Pearl, L. (2000) 'Experience and knowledge of young people regarding illicit drug use, 1969-99', *Addiction,* 95(8): 1225-35.

RDS Publications

Requests for Publications

Copies of our publications and a list of those currently available may be obtained from:

Home Office
Research, Development and Statistics Directorate
Communications Development Unit
Room 201, Home Office
50 Queen Anne's Gate
London SW1H 9AT
Telephone: 020 7273 2084 (answerphone outside of office hours)
Facsimile: 020 7222 0211
E-mail: publications.rds@homeoffice.gsi.gov.uk

alternatively

why not visit the RDS website at
          Internet: http://www.homeoffice.gov.uk/rds/index.html

where many of our publications are available to be read on screen or downloaded for printing.